VIOLIN
REPERTOIRE

DVOŘÁK
SONATINA in G major, op.100
for violin and piano
Edited by Yuriko KURONUMA

ドヴォルジャーク
ソナティーナ ト長調 Op.100

黒沼ユリ子 監修

音楽之友社

JN248699

ONGAKU NO TOMO EDITION

今この楽譜を手にされている方がたへ

黒沼ユリ子

❧ 作曲家名表記について

この曲を演奏される前に、少し私からお伝えしたいことがあります。まず第一に、私はこの曲の作曲家の名前の日本語表記の歴史を覆して、ドヴォルジャックでもドボルザークでもなくドヴォルジャークとしたことです。

何しろチェコ語という言語は、日本語とあまりにも発音がかけ離れていて、それをカタカナで書き表すことは不可能に近いのではなく、本当に不可能なのです。すでに気づかれているとは思いますが、このDvořákという名前の中のrの上に小さなvに似た印が付いている文字の音は日本語のみならず、ヨーロッパの他の言語のどれにも存在していません。チェコ語独特の音なのです。řと書かれた文字は、ル［R］を発音しながら同時にジュという音も絡ませて発音する文字なのです。これをちゃんと発音できるようになるまでに私がどのくらいの月日の時間を捧げたかは記憶にありませんが、とても難しかったことだけは確かです。

ドイツ人やアメリカ人はこの印を平気で無視してドヴォラックとかドヴォラークと読んでいますが、日本では少しでも原語に近い発音にしようと、おそらくチェコ人の発音に耳を傾け、ドヴォルジャックとかドボルザークにしたのでしょう。Dvořákの中のaがáとなっているのは、単に長く伸ばす意味しかありませんが、řの方は、日本ではこれまで、例えばJiříという名前をイルジーと表記していたのですが、この頃は、それをイージーとするようになりました。でも私は「それではあまりにもřを無視しすぎている」と思うのでルを小さな文字にしてドヴォルジャークとすることにしたのです。つまりRを強調しないこの方が、少なくともドヴォルジャックよりはチェコ語の発音に近くなると考えたからです。

ですがもう一点、チェコ語をどうしても日本語では完全に表記するのが不可能である原因が、カタカナにあることも知っておいてください。

カタカナの50音の中に子音だけの文字は最後のンしかありませんが、チェコ語には子音のみがいくつも繋がる語が少なくないのです。日本語の50音では、カキクケコから先の全ての子音は母音のアイウエオが同時に発音されてしまうからです。ですからDvořákを発音する場合も、はじめの2字［DとV］は子音が二つ繋がっているので、ドヴォではなく、ドからオを省いてDVOと発音してください。でもカタカナでの表記では、どうしてもドとせざるを得ないのが現実です。

「こんな些細なこと」と思われる方もあるでしょうが、少なくとも「音」の専門家を自認する音楽家のみなさんには知っていて頂きたいのです。

❧ 作品名表記について

第二に、私はこの曲のタイトルを、通常使われている「ソナチネ」ではなく「ソナティーナ」としました。チェコ語の原譜にはもちろんSONATINAと書かれているからです。しかし日本で「ソナチネ」と呼ばれている曲から浮かぶイメージには、どうしても「子供たちが最初に出会う曲」という印象があることをぬぐいきれません。

SONATINAとは、「小さなSONATA」または「短いソナタ」という意味で「ソナタ」には違いないのです。一般に作曲家たちが「ソナタ」というタイトルを選んで発想するとき、そこには何か重要な自らの思いを語りたいというような意思があるものなのです。ではドヴォルジャークがこの「ソナティーナ」に託した気持ちとはどんなことだったのでしょうか？

それを理解するためには、彼の生涯についてを少しでも紐解く必要がありますが、せめてこの曲が作曲された同じ年に生まれた、彼の他の作品、かの有名な交響曲第9番「新世界より」や弦楽四重奏曲作品96の「アメリカ」に耳を傾けてみて下さい。この「ソナティーナ」と比較しながら聴いてみると、ある共通点が聴こえて来るはずです。

なぜなら、この年がドヴォルジャークの生涯の他の時代と比べて、際立って異なっているからです。彼が祖国を遠く離れたアメリカ大陸に渡り、そこで生まれた作品という意味において。

❧ 新世界にて

この前年の1892年11月に、妻のアンナと子供たち二人のみ（長女と長男）を伴ってドヴォルジャークはアメリカ・ナショナル音楽院の校長として新大陸の大都会・ニューヨークに到着していました。

ボヘミア（現在のチェコ）の首都プラハからさほど遠くないネラホゼヴェスという寒村に生まれ育ったドヴォルジャークにとって、大西洋を船で横断してニューヨークに移住するという決心をしたこと自体が、今日でしたら「宇宙ステーションに赴く」くらいの驚嘆すべきことだったのです。

それは、プラハの小さな楽団でヴィオラを弾いたり、個人の家でピアノの出稽古をしたり、教会の臨時オルガニストとして貧しい生活を送っていた時代のドヴォルジャークには、全く夢想だにできなかったことでしたから。

「稀にみる豊かな才能を持つ若き作曲家」としてブラームスからベルリンの楽譜出版社ジムロックに紹介されてやっと世に出られた時、彼はすでに32歳で、幸せな新婚生活を送っていましたが、その数年後に、疫病や事故死と思われる原因

によって次つぎと最初に授かった3人の子供たちの死と直面させられます。悲しみのどん底に落とされた夫妻にとっての唯一の救いの道は、十字架から降ろされたキリストを抱く聖母マリアの悲しみと自分たちのそれを重ね合わせることしか、考えられなかったのです。そうして生まれたのがオラトリオ「スターバト・マーテル（悲しみの聖母）」でした。それはイギリスをはじめヨーロッパ中で大成功を博し、その後の彼の歩む道をますます広げ、遂にはケンブリッジ大学から「名誉音楽博士号」まで授与されることになったのです。そんなドヴォルジャークだったからこそ、その2年後にはニューヨークに招かれたのでした。

　幼いころからチェコ民族の歌や踊りに囲まれて育ち、ボヘミアの（つまりドイツ語でチェコのこと）ゆるやかな野と山を愛し、故郷を思う気持ちは誰にも負けないほど深かったドヴォルジャークでしたから、異国にあって抱いた望郷の念は、多くの彼の手紙に残されている言葉の行間に滲んでいるように、とても深いものでした。それが音楽になって表現されているのが、この3曲、つまり交響曲「新世界より」と弦楽四重奏曲「アメリカ」であり、このヴァイオリンとピアノのための「ソナティーナ」なのです。

❦ ソナティーナ

　これら3曲は共にアメリカに引っ越した翌年の1893年に生まれた作品で、「新世界より」は1月から5月にかけてニューヨークで、「アメリカ」は、プラハに残してきた4人の子供たちも到着してやっと家族全員が合流した夏に、アイオワ州のスピルヴィルというチェコ移民たちの村で、そしてこの「ソナティーナ」は、楽しかった子供たちとの夏休みの歓びを思い出しつつ、秋になってからニューヨークの自宅で作曲されたのでした。

　この3作品のどの曲にも共通するテーマは、アメリカでの新しい生活への不安と同時にさまざまな新体験の歓び、遠い祖国を想う気持ち、踊りの楽しさ、そして常に忘れることのなかった「神への感謝の念」が謳われていることではないでしょうか。

　そしてこの「ソナティーナ」で驚かされる点は、各楽章の最後の終止線の後に作曲された日付が記されていることです。
　第1楽章は11月24日に、第2楽章と第3楽章はたった1日後の25日に、そして第4楽章のみは少し間がおかれて12月3日でしたが、これもたった1日で完成されているのです。まさに、過ぎ去った夏休みの日記を読み返しながらペンを走らせたかのようで、その情景さえ目に浮かぶようです。

　第1楽章は、6人の子供たちがプラハから到着して、家族全員が揃った喜びの声が聞こえるよう。
　第2楽章は、のちに20世紀の名ヴァイオリニスト、フリッツ・クライスラーによって「インディアン・ラメント（インディアンの哀しみ）」というタイトルの小品に作りかえられたので、そちらの方がこの原曲よりも有名になってしまった感がぬぐいきれませんが、悲哀に満ちたこの楽章は、私にはむしろその数日前の11月7日に新聞のニュースで知ったチャイコフスキーの訃報が、彼の脳裏から一瞬も離れなかったのではないかと思えるのです。彼とは、ほんの1歳しかちがいませんでしたが、作曲家としては大先輩のチャイコフスキーが、後輩のドヴォルジャークを大親友として扱ってくれていたことを、彼はかけがえのない喜びとして感謝していたのですから。曲の中間部では、まるで二人が楽しい思い出を語り合っているかのような姿も目に浮かんできますが、この楽章は「寂しい永遠のお別れの挨拶」ではないかという思いが、私には感じられてならないのです。

　にもかかわらず、この同じ日に作曲された第3楽章の方は、また何と明るく、楽しさにあふれているのでしょう。まさに子供たちが公園の木陰で遊び、カクレンボでもしているかのような情景さえ見えるようではありませんか？
　そして最終の第4楽章。つねに前向きで、肯定的な精神の持ち主であったドヴォルジャークではありましたが、12月に入り、いよいよニューヨークの楽壇に自分の真価が問われる時が近いことを忘れてはいなかったのでしょう。そう、あのカーネギーホールでの交響曲「新世界より」の世界初演が、近づいていたのです。それは16日と決まっていました。ヨーロッパの楽壇では今や押しも押されもしない大作曲家と認められていたドヴォルジャークではありましたが、多少の不安もあり、それに打ち勝ちたいような気持ちがこの楽章の中央部に短調であらわれているようでもあり、それを懐かしい故郷を思い浮かべることで気分を落ち着かせたりしていたのかも知れません。でも結局、あたかも「バンザーイ」をしているかのような大勝利で、歓喜に満ちた表情でこの楽章は終わっており、それは同時にこの「ソナティーナ」の全曲の終わりでもあるのです。

　まるでこの「ソナティーナ」に運を賭けていたかのような、彼のこの楽観的な予測は見事に命中、「新世界より」の成功はカーネギーホール開館以来とも言われたほどの大ニュースになりました。

　1893年12月16日以来、この「チェコの一介の音楽家」と自称していたアントニーン・ドヴォルジャークの名前と交響曲「新世界より」は、人類の宝もののリストに入り、不滅の音楽になったのです。

Preface

Yuriko Kuronuma

The term 'sonatina' implies a small or short sonata without detracting from the fact that works in this form are still very much sonatas. Generally speaking, when a composer employs the term 'sonata' as the title of a work, he wishes to convey his own important and distinctive ideas in the work. What then were the ideas and feelings that Dvořák strove to get across in his *Sonatina*?

In order to understand this, we need to take a look at Dvořák's own life and career. In particular we need to listen to other works that he composed at around this time, notably the Symphony No. 9, *'From the New World'* and the String Quartet op.96, *'American'*. Listening to the *Sonatina* in the context of these other works, various shared features soon become apparent. Including these three, all the works that Dvořák composed in 1893 differ markedly in character from those dating from other years. This is because this year was itself markedly different from other periods in Dvořák's life, being the year when he left his motherland to travel to far-away America, where he composed these works.

✻ From the New World
It was in November 1892 that Dvořák, together with his wife Anna and a son and daughter, arrived in the grand New World city of New York, where Dvořák was to take up the position of director of the National Conservatory of Music of America.

Dvořák was born in the small village of Nelahozeves close to the Bohemian capital of Prague. For someone from such a background, the very idea of travelling across the Atlantic must have been as daunting as the idea of us today going off to live in a space station. For Dvořák, who had previously played the viola in a small Prague orchestra as well as giving piano lessons in private homes and occasionally playing the organ in church, this was a turn of events that he could scarcely have envisaged until then.

Dvořák at last began to make a name for himself when Brahms, who considered him to be a 'young composer of rich and rarely seen talent', recommended him to the Berlin music publisher Simrock. At this time Dvořák was already 32 years old and happily married, but in the ensuing years he was faced by the loss through illness and accident of his first three children. The only relief provided to the despondent composer and his wife was the image of the Virgin Mary's sadness when her son, Jesus Christ, was lowered into her arms from the cross. This was the background to the *Stabat Mater* oratorio. The work proved to be a great success throughout Europe and especially in England.

Dvořák's career subsequently expanded by leaps and bounds until he was awarded an honorary doctorate by the University of Cambridge. This development in his career led to his receipt and acceptance of an invitation to come to New York two years later.

Dvořák grew up surrounded by Czech folk song and dance and with a strong attachment to the gentle woods and mountains of his native Bohemia. His love for his homeland was indeed second to none, and the profound sense of nostalgia and homesickness that he felt when faced by life in a totally foreign environment is conveyed between the lines in the many letters that he wrote while in America. These feelings revealed themselves in music mainly in three major works, the Symphony No. 9, *'From the New World'*, the String Quartet op.96, *'American'*, and the *Sonatina* for violin and piano.

✻ Sonatina in G major, op.100
These three works date from 1893, the year after Dvořák had moved to America. He composed the *New World Symphony* in New York between January and May and the *'American'* string quartet in the Czech immigrant village of Spillville in Iowa in the summer of that year, after being joined in America by his whole family, including the four children he had initially left behind in Prague. Inspiration for the *Sonatina* came to him that autumn at home in New York. Dvořák composed the work to express the happiness he had felt at having been able to spend the summer holidays with his children.

The themes that run through all three works are the unease that Dvořák felt with regard to his new life in America in ambiguous combination with the joy of exposure to all kinds of new experiences, nostalgic feelings towards his distant homeland, the pleasures of dancing, and the sense of thanks to God that constitutes the current underlying his oeuvre as a whole.

An unusual feature of the score of the *Sonatina* is that the final double barline of each movement is followed by the date of composition. The first movement shows the date 24 November and the second and third movements are dated 25 November. The fourth movement is marked with the slightly later date of 3 December, and also appears to have been composed on a single day. One can imagine Dvořák filling out his manuscript paper as he read through his diary records of the recently passed summer holidays.

The first movement seems to convey the joy that Dvořák must have felt after the arrival from Prague of his six children and the gathering of the whole family in America.

The second movement was adapted by the great 20th-century violinist Fritz Kreisler in the form of a piece entitled *Indian Lament*. Kreisler's adaptation has if anything become more well known than Dvořák's original work, but it seems to me that the pathos inherent in the original work suggests that the sad news of Tchaikovsky's death that had appeared in the newspaper a few weeks earlier on 7 November was still fresh in Dvořák's mind. Tchaikovsky was only one year older than Dvořák, but Dvořák thought of him as a father figure and was enormously grateful for the friendship that Tchaikovsky bestowed upon him. The central section of the piece conjures up the image of the two composers engaged in animated conversation. Personally, I find it impossible to shake off the image of this piece as a sad message of final farewell.

Nevertheless, the third movement of the *Sonatina*, which was composed on the same day as the second movement, is full of a sense of brightness and joy that evokes the image of the composer's children playing hide-and-seek amidst the trees in a park.

The fourth movement was composed in December when Dvořák, who adopted a positive attitude to everything he did, was faced with the imminent première of a work that would make or break his reputation in the New York musical world. The work in question was of course the *New World Symphony*, which was due to receive its world première at the Carnegie Hall on 16 December. By this time Dvořák had established an unassailable reputation for himself in the European musical world, but his lingering sense of insecurity about his reputation seems to have manifested itself in the use of the minor key in the central section of this movement. Perhaps it was by thinking nostalgically of his homeland that he managed to regain his composure. In contrast, the movement and the work as a whole end on a joyful and victorious tone.

Although it might be regarded as tempting fate, the prescient optimism of *Sonatina* was fully justified: the première of the *'New World' Symphony* proved to be one of the greatest ever successes in the history of the Carnegie Hall.

Ever since its first performance on 16 December 1893, the *'New World' Symphony* by Antonín Dvořák, who was apt to refer to himself as an 'insignificant Czech musician', has entered the roster of the immortal treasures of humankind.

(Translation: Robin Thompson)

記号一覧 / Glossary

少しゆったり	~	Slightly relaxed
ごくわずかに一息入れて、次を新たに	/	Take a breather very slightly before beginning again
一息入れて、次を新たに	,	Take a breather before beginning again
弓の先で、又は先から	tip	Play at or from the tip of the bow
弓の元で、又は元から	frog	Play at or from the frog of the bow
弓の中ほどから	middle	Play from around the middle of the bow
わずかな弓で	poco arco	
半分の弓で	half bow	
全弓で	full bow	

本版は、Simrock社の初版楽譜を底本とし、音量やアーティキュレーションなどの演奏表現に関わる記号を監修者の解釈のもとに記した実用版楽譜です。

This edition is based on the original first edition published by Simrock. It is intended to serve as a performing edition with the dynamics, articulation and other markings added by the editor in accordance with her own interpretation of the work.

SONATINA
I

Allegro risoluto

Antonín Dvořák, Op. 100

* 第3、第11小節は、ボウイングが逆でも同じ表情のアクセントで。 　　* Although the bowing is opposite in bars 3 and 11, the phrase should be played with the same expressive accents.

* 1. は、好みによって割愛し 2. に進んでもよい。 *The passage enclosed in 1. may be omitted in order to proceed directly to 2.

*冒頭と異なり短調になっている意味を表情に乗せる。つまり少々懐疑的に。

* The change to the minor key should be highlighted expressively in a questioning tone in order to form a contrast with the opening section.

24. 11. 1893

II

*初版譜には Meno mosso, Tempo I と表示されていますが、これはここまでのヴァイオリンパートのリズムをピアノが受け持ち（聞き役）、ヴァイオリンが語り出す訳で、同じテンポで続けるべきだと思い L'istesso Tempo としました。

* The first edition bears the indication *Meno mosso, Tempo I*, but I have taken the liberty of changing this marking to *L'istesso tempo*. This is because the rhythm in the violin part up to this point is supported passively by the piano with the violin a declamatory mode, suggesting that the music needs to continue at the same tempo.

25. 11. 1893

VIOLIN
REPERTOIRE

DVOŘÁK
SONATINA in G major, op.100
for violin and piano
Edited by Yuriko KURONUMA

ドヴォルジャーク
ソナティーナ ト長調 Op.100

黒沼ユリ子 監修

Violin

音楽之友社

ONGAKU NO TOMO EDITION

*冒頭と異なり短調になっている意味を表情に乗せる。つまり少々懐疑的に。

* The change to the minor key should be highlighted expressively in a questioning tone in order to form a contrast with the opening section.

24. 11. 1893

II

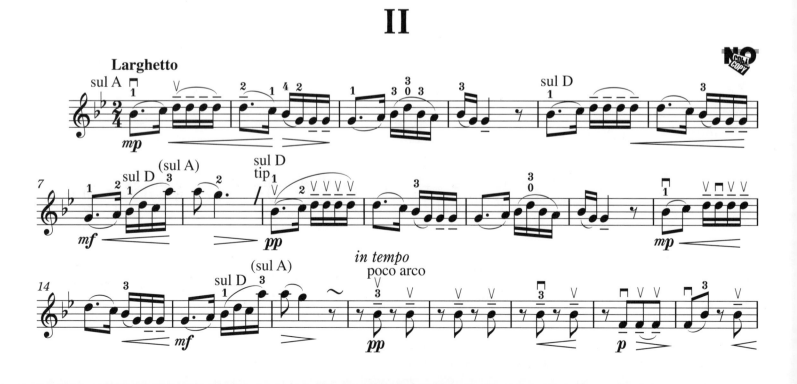

25. 11. 1893

---

* 初版譜には Meno mosso, Tempo I と表示 されていますが、これはここまでのヴァイオリンパートのリズムを ピアノが受け持ち（聞き役）、ヴァイオリンが語り出す訳で、同じテンポ で続けるべきだと思い L'istesso Tempo としました。

* The first edition bears the indication *Meno mosso, Tempo I*, but I have taken the liberty of changing this marking to *L'istesso tempo*. This is because the rhythm in the violin part up to this point is supported passively by the piano with the violin a declamatory mode, suggesting that the music needs to continue at the same tempo.

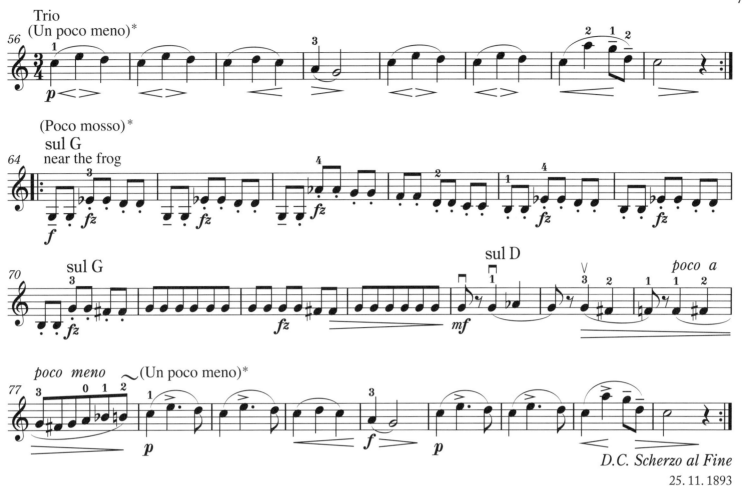

* Trio は A－B－A の三部形式になっていますが、A は少しゆったりした部分、B は元気を取り戻して演奏する部分です。

* The trio is in ternary (A-B-A) form, with the A section being relaxed and the B section regaining momentum.

IV

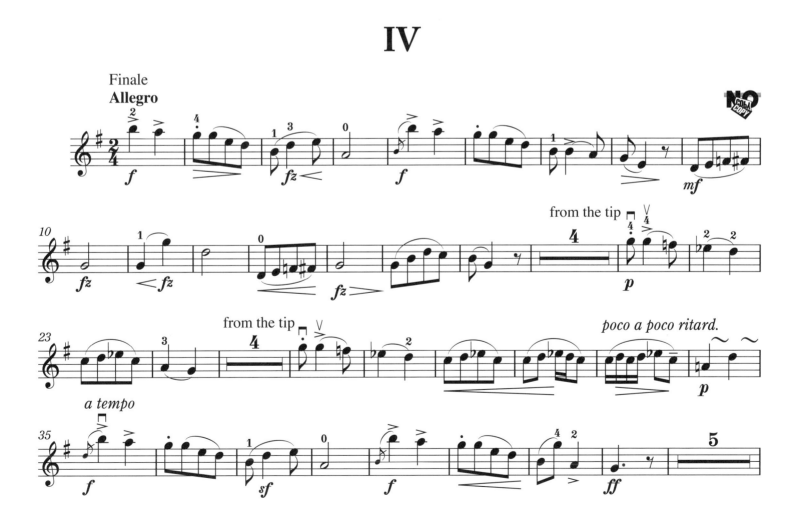

*これらのフラジョレットをよく響かせて fz で。 * These harmonics should be brought out clearly by being played fz.

* Trio は A-B-A の三部形式になっていますが、A は少しゆっ
たりした部分、B は元気を取り戻して演奏する部分です。

* The trio is in ternary (A-B-A) form, with the A section
being relaxed and the B section regaining momentum.

25. 11. 1893

IV

*これらのフラジョレットをよく響かせて *fz* で。　*These harmonics should be brought out clearly by being played *fz*.

作品を演奏するということ

黒沼ユリ子

ある作品の「演奏」とは、決して楽譜通りに音符を音にすることではないのです。その作品の生まれた陰にあったすべての状況を理解し共感してこそ、初めてその演奏が聴く者の心に届く「音楽演奏」・インタープリテーションになるのではないかと私は思うのです。それは20世紀の演劇を19世紀の演出法から革命的に飛躍させたロシアの「スタニスラフスキー・システムに似て」とも言えるかもしれません。

そして「音楽演奏を聴く行為」とは、それによって、聴く者を作曲者の気持ちと自分のとを重ね合わせて共感すること、のみではなく、自分を「非日常的な空間」に飛翔させることを可能にすること、でもあるのではないでしょうか？

「ある演奏」を聴いた後の感想は、それを聴いた人の数と同数あって当然、とも言えるでしょう。

文字では書けない、言葉でも言い表せない人間の感情を、音楽というものによって、作曲者のペンを通じて、そして演奏者の橋渡しによる「演奏」によって、聴く者に伝えることができた時、それこそを「演奏芸術」と言えるのではないでしょうか。

Performing a musical work

Yuriko Kuronuma

Performance of a musical work is not simply a matter of performing the notes as they appear on the written page. I believe that it's only when the performer understands and is in sympathy with all the factors and conditions that underpin a particular work that it's possible to give a truly musical performance, that is to say an interpretation that is able to capture the hearts of listeners. This is an approach similar to that of the Russian Stanislavsky system which revolutionised theatrical performance, breaking away from 19th-century methods to create a new style of 20th-century stage art.

The act of listening to a musical performance in this mould should enable listeners to develop a sympathetic understanding of the composer's own feelings as well as transporting them to a dimension outside the realm of the mundane.

It is only natural that the number of impressions gained from listening to a particular musical performance should be equivalent to the number of listeners to the performance.

The true art of performance comes about when human emotions inexpressible in writing or in speech are conveyed to the listener through the pen of the composer with the performer acting as the bridge between composer and listener.

(Translation: Robin Thompson)

演奏へのアドヴァイス

黒沼ユリ子

――― 第 1 楽 章 ―――

音楽には常に会話があることを忘れないように！ 例えば冒頭の4小節と次の4小節などでは、語っている人が異なる、つまり対話をしているように。

Advice on performance

Yuriko Kuronuma

――― **First movement** ―――

Never forget that the music features an ongoing dialogue! For instance, the opening four bars are followed by four bars in which the 'speakers' in the dialogue are different.

そして17小節目からは今度は二人が「そうねぇー」という風に同調しながら話をしているようではありませんか？

From Bar 17 onwards we get the impression of the two speakers conversing together in full agreement.

37小節からは一方の話に相手が相槌を打っているように……。

From Bar 37 one speaker seems to be giving assent to the other.

52小節からは「そうだ」「そうだ」と二人の意見が合って60小節に到達。

From Bars 52 to 60 the two speakers seem to be again affirming each other's opinions.

2楽章

この楽章は、フリッツ・クライスラーの小品「インディアン・ラメント」のタイトルによってあたかも、ドヴォルジャークがそれを認めていたかのように誰もがこのタイトルを疑問に思わないようですが、私には親友チャイコフスキーとの別れの曲、別れの悲しみの独白のように思えるのです。少し速く（Poco più mosso）の部分は、チャイコフスキーがドヴォルジャークに思い出話を語り、ドヴォルジャークが「そう、そう、そうでしたね」とでも云っているようです。ですから、56小節目からはヴァイオリンとピアノの立場が逆になった続きなので、ここではテンポの変更（meno mosso）は無しです。

Second movement

Due to the title *Indian Lament* given to this movement by Fritz Kreisler, it is generally assumed that Dvořák composed this piece with American Indians in mind and little doubt has been cast upon this assumption. However, it seems to me to be more appropriate to consider the piece as a lament in the form of a soliloquy featuring an expression of sad farewell to the Dvořák's recently deceased close friend Tchaikovsky. The *poco più mosso* section seems to convey Dvořák's memories of Tchaikovsky in a consistent tone of reflective affirmation. The passage from bar 56 is a continuation of the section in which the respective positions of the violin and the piano, and there is therefore no change in tempo to meno mosso at this point.

第3楽章

この楽章は、まさに子供たちが、公園の木の陰に隠れて「かくれん坊」をしているような情景を思い浮かべながら演奏して下さい。冒頭からの8小節はヤブの中に小さくなって隠れていると、9小節目で「いたぞー、見つけたぁー」と言われているようではありませんか？

Third movement

This movement should be performed with the image of children playing hide-and-seek amidst the trees in a park in mind. The first eight bars suggest a child hiding in the undergrowth and being discovered by the other children playing the game from the ninth bar onwards.

そして17小節目からは皆が一緒になって飛び回っているうちに再び誰かがだんだん隠れだし（37、38、39）、40小節目でまた冒頭のようなかくれん坊をしているみたいです。

From Bar 17 we get the impression of children dashing around before once again going off to hide (Bars 37 to 39), with the opening game beginning once again at Bar 40.

第4楽章 / Fourth movement

第4楽章で私がつけた最大の変更は、冒頭を **mp** や **p** ではなく、元気よく、自信を持った態度の **f** でスタートしたいということ。この夏にやっと子供たち全6人が両親と合流し、楽しかったドヴォルジャーク・ファミリーの雰囲気を出したいので。

The most significant change I've made in the fourth movement is to the dynamics markings at the start of the piece. Instead of the piano marking, I've indicated that the movement should be begun energetically with a forte dynamic because of my wish to recreate the happy mood of the Dvořák family, with parents and all six children finally able to gather together in the summer of the year in which the work was composed.

でも62小節からはまるで皆がプラハやヴィソカー（作曲をしていた森の家）のことなどを心配しているかのようでもあります。または、2週間足らず後に控えた交響曲第9番「新世界より」の世界初演とその結果を少々心配していたのかもしれません。

But from Bar 62 we get the impression of the family directing their thoughts wistfully back to Prague and the house in the woods in the village of Výsoká, where Dvořák did much of his creative work. This may well also have been a time when Dvořák was concerned about the imminent world première of the Symphony No. 9, 'From the New World'.

でも、106小節の Molto tranquillo では、チェコの緩やかな丘に広がる農地と点在する森の景色が浮かんで、皆で懐かしんでいるのかしら……。

The *Molto tranquillo* passage at Bar 106 evokes the nostalgic image of fields, meadows and forest landscapes among the gently undulating hills of Bohemia.

そして150小節の Tempo I からは、いろいろ心配事も思い出し、家族で意見もいろいろ出たり……。そして再び冒頭のテーマが現れて類似場面が繰り返され126小節からコーダに向かいます。

Various concerns reappear with the reappearance of *Tempo I* at Bar 150, with each family member expressing their own opinions. The opening theme then reappears and a similar scene is repeated, with the music moving towards the coda at Bar 126.

331小節目のトリルは、最初ゆっくり、少しずつ速くして通常のトリルにしながら、どんどんと肯定的、楽観的な結末に向かって走り去るようにして、この曲全体の幕を閉じます。「新世界より」の大成功に確信を持って臨んでいるように聴こえませんか？

The trill at Bar 331 should begin slowly and gradually increase in speed until the normal speed is reached. The work as a whole ends after a headlong rush towards its positive, optimistic conclusion, perhaps reflecting Dvořák's confidence in the success of the forthcoming première of the *'New World' Symphony*.

(Translation: Robin Thompson)

黒沼ユリ子

小学5年生で全国学生音楽コンクールにて第1位ならびに文部大臣賞を受賞。桐朋学園高校音楽科1年の時、日本音楽コンクールで第1位ならびに特賞を受け、17歳でW.ロイブナー指揮NHK交響楽団とデビュー。18歳でヨーロッパへ留学し、プラハ音楽芸術アカデミーを首席で卒業。同アカデミー在学中の1960年、プラハ現代音楽演奏コンクールで第1位。1962年「プラハの春」国際音楽祭にてM.トルノフスキ指揮プラハ交響楽団とヨーロッパ・デビュー。以来、国際的なソリストとして世界各地で活動。S.コミッシオーナ、C.チャベス、M.ヤンソンス、E.クルツ、K.マズア、E.マータ、V.ノイマン、M.ショスタコーヴィチ、G.ロジェストヴェンスキーほか著名な指揮者やオーケストラと共演。1979年に本邦初演を行った廣瀬量平のヴァイオリン協奏曲を、1981年にはニューヨークのカーネギーホールでアメリカ交響楽団と、その後はメキシコやチェコなど各国で、初演を続ける。

1980年メキシコ・シティーに弦楽器の音楽院「アカデミア・ユリコ・クロヌマ」を開校。同校は2012年6月に社会情勢の変化に伴って32年間の活動に幕を引くまでの間、国際的なソリストとして活躍中のヴァイオリニスト、アドリアン・ユストゥスを筆頭に、メキシコ国内でオーケストラのコンサートマスターやメンバー、室内楽奏者や教師として活躍する数十名のプロのヴァイオリニスト、アメリカ、カナダ、フランス、日本で活躍する元・生徒など数多くの人材を輩出。また、多くのアマチュア弦楽器奏者および聴衆を育てたことで高く評価されている。同校の生徒たちの訪日による1985年から4回にわたる全国各地での「日本・メキシコ友好コンサート」公演や、元・生徒や教師たちによる弦楽合奏団「ソリスタス・メヒコ・ハポン」の2010年の来日公演などを通じて両国の友好の絆を一層強めた。

これまでに多数のLP、CD、著書を発表。ドヴォルジャークに関連するものには、本作を収めたCD「黒沼ユリ子の世界——ドヴォルジャーク、スーク、フォーレを弾く」（1989年、FONTEC）、CD「チェコ・ヴァイオリン音楽選」（2016年、ビクターエンタテインメント）、書籍「わが祖国チェコの大地よ——ドヴォルジャーク物語」（1982年、リブリオ出版）などがある。

Yuriko Kuronuma

Yuriko Kuronuma was awarded first prize and the Prize of the Minister of Education at the Student Music Competition of Japan at the age of ten. As a first-year student at the senior high school attached to Toho Gakuen College Music Department she was awarded first prize in the Japan Music Competition, after which she made her debut at the age of seventeen with the NHK Symphony Orchestra directed by Wilhelm Loibner. She travelled to Europe to study at the age of eighteen and graduated with top honours from the National Academy of Musical Arts in Prague. While still studying in Prague she gained first prize at the Prague Competition of Contemporary Musical Interpretation. She made her European debut at the 1962 Prague Spring International Festival with the Prague Symphony Orchestra directed by Martin Turnovsky, since when she has been active worldwide as a soloist. She has performed with many orchestras under the batons of conductors including Sergiu Comissiona, Carlos Chávez, Mariss Jansons, Efrem Kurtz, Kurt Masur, Eduardo Mata, Václav Neumann, Maxim Shostakovich and Gennady Rozhdestvensky. In 1979 she gave the first performance of the Violin Concerto by Ryōhei Hirose, followed by a performance of the same work with the American Symphony Orchestra in New York in 1981 and subsequent performances in Mexico and Czechoslovakia.

In 1980 she founded the Academia Yuriko Kuronuma, a music school for string players, in Mexico City. Due to changes in the social environment, in June 2012 she closed the school after 32 years during which she trained several dozen violinists who subsequently became leading professionals including the international soloist Adrian Justus and many violinists who are currently active in Mexico as concertmasters, orchestral performers, chamber music specialists and teachers. Her pupils also include violinists active in the United States, Canada, France and Japan. Her work as instructor of amateur string players and audiences is also highly regarded. Pupils of the Academia Yuriko Kuronuma visited Japan on four occasions, for the first time in 1985, giving 'Japan-Mexico Friendship Concerts' all over the country. The Solistas Mexico-Japon string ensemble consisting of former pupils and teachers of the Academy helped to cement the links of friendship between the two nations through performances given on their visit to Japan in 2010.

ドヴォルジャーク　ソナティーナ　ト長調　Op.100

2018年1月31日　第1刷発行

監修者　黒沼ユリ子
発行者　堀内久美雄
発行所　東京都新宿区神楽坂6の30
　　　　株式会社 音楽之友社
　　　　電話 03(3235)2111(代)　〒162-8716
　　　　振替 00170-4-196250
　　　　http://www.ongakunotomo.co.jp/

476660

© 2018 by ONGAKU NO TOMO SHA CORP., Tokyo, Japan.

本書の全部または一部のコピー、スキャン、デジタル化等の無断複製は著作権法上での例外を除き禁じられています。また、購入者以外の代行業者等、第三者による本書のスキャンやデジタル化は、たとえ個人や家庭内での利用であっても著作権法上認められておりません。

楽譜浄書：加賀屋浄書
装丁：吉原順一
翻訳：ロビン・トンプソン
印刷／製本：(株) 平河工業社